Dreaming in Italics

Emily Holtom

BookLeaf Publishing

India | USA | UK

Author Photograph by Briony Canning.

Presentation by *BookLeaf Publishing*

Web: www.bookleafpub.com

E-mail: info@bookleafpub.com

ISBN: 978-93-5744-356-2

First edition 2022

DEDICATION

For my family

ACKNOWLEDGEMENT

Given that this book was created in secret, it seems odd to be writing out Thank You's when it was a project of completely independent undertaking. So, these are the acknowledgements that you never saw coming.

Firstly, to my amazing family. You inspire me every day with your collective strength and endless love. I love you all £17.

To my closest and most wonderful friends, (of which there are too many of you to name!), thank you for not being weird about my whole literature obsession, and keeping me smiling even when you didn't realize that I was crashing into writer's block.

I also owe a ridiculous amount of this collection to all the amazing creatives from the On Your Doorstep collective, without whom I couldn't have dared to pick my pen back up. Special mention to Scarlett, whose writing is equally beautiful as it is inspirational – thank you for everything!

Thank you to everyone at BookLeaf for letting me turn my frantic scribbles and brain dumps into an actual, physical book – even writing that seems completely surreal.

Finally, there is never a more rewarding experience than dotting the final I and crossing the final T to a finished poem, but being able to do these things for an entire published collection is something different altogether. So, my final thank you is to any reader that decided to pick up my little book and give it a flick through in the first place – you have made one poet incredibly happy.

PREFACE

You don't need to be a poet to find comfort in poetry.
James Gates Percival once said, 'The world is full of poetry. The air is living with its spirit; and the waves dance to the music of its melodies, and sparkle in its brightness'. We all seek comfort and calm from such unique sources, but even in that small act there is beautiful lyricism.

Abstract poetry, that is to say poetry which at face value often seems nonsensical and arbitrary, can feel particularly out of reach to those just entering into this form of literature, so my advice to you is this:
Don't make sense of the words or try to read them like you used to dissect Shakespeare plays at school – feel them. Whether that's in the shape that your lips make as you read aloud, or the speed of the little commentary from inside your head, poetry is there to be enjoyed, not a thing over which to get confused or stressed. How you experience a poem depends entirely on your own rhythms – your mood, what you have experienced that day, perhaps even your very environment – it is not something that can be explained or reduced to a couple of quick

sentences. Some poems in this collection may in fact offer up their meaning readily in less abstract forms, while others might always remain slightly foggy to you. You may find that more of it gets uncovered the more times you read it, and that is really the beauty of this abstract form: being able to relive the same few words in entirely new ways.

So, rather than stressing when the meaning doesn't come to you immediately, just enjoy the artform as it is, whether that be with the poems from this or another collection entirely. The reader is the one to make the words come to life, give them meaning, and add their own form of lyricism, and this is an entirely individual adventure. What your mind takes away from the reading experience will likely be totally different to the next. As Maya Angelou said, 'Words mean more than what is set down on paper. It takes the human voice to infuse them with deeper meaning'.

We are all of us poets, but I am lucky enough to have been able to put my words onto the page. So, if you have so much as accidentally picked up Dreaming in Italics and aimlessly flicked your eyes over to a random stanza, then I hope you find enjoyment here, however the words present themselves to you. If even a single line affords you some escapism, then the poetry has done what it was made for.

Intensely Too Late//

On the shoreline of a mourning decade, I fell in
love with a memory.
I have known that the chaos fizzes from the way
you abandon yourself—
That streak over your soul that chases an
afterthought.
In those spaces between the seconds
My mind, a disorganised room, collects on you
Waiting to consume what isn't.

Sigh//

It always happens this way.
Little but saturated sighs escape through the
echo
       of sand in an hourglass
       coaxed accidentally into falling.
I've seen how flames dance on the edge of your
tongue like this,
Pearlising the darkness
In deep shades of wine   and would.
You are the coffee stain pressed between heavy
novels and stored,
The clumsy whims
And lyrical escapades of myself.
You are music with a hand over its mouth,
The same problem in a different font.

You've always lived at an off-angle, and
In this panorama of bruised knees and belly
aches,
I'm thinking there's time I have yet to explore.
If I dream about you now—
       Remind me not to.

All's Fair//

The last conversation we had, we stood on the
merry-go-round of exile in confusion.
There was,
but there will be,
might be
another way to bend the scribbles and scaffold
as if two worlds colliding could make anything
more than 90s classics
on the corny boulevards where love never was.
You whispered to me in candy floss tones
          and dodged
every why how when with who
wondering that you've never tasted this before.

Family//

The teapot is a warped and fragile thing.
Deep valleys fracture the clay that once was
smooth and proud
And the shattered pieces have been pushed back
into place too often to count.
But my hands are steady as I pour—
      There is always glue for next time.

As My Soul Slips On//

5

This time, I have abandoned my body to new
adventures,
Seeking passage on a bumblebee's wing
And slipping through the unfathomable space
between a spider's web.
I will bruise the clouds
Simply for the pleasure of watching them colour
Until I can no longer feel the keen sting
Of soiled memories jerking my sleeves.

Visions of Stolen Dreams//

November is warm in your hands.
I let you coax the amber from my tongue
And pluck music from outdated heartstrings
That can be folded away as if into an old
newspaper.
The ink has long since run,
The pages curling with frail abandonment,
But I read your music like the most exquisite
novel.

How do you wade so unaffected
Into the torrent of what might be?
It is the colour of things better said in
whispers—
Rather,
It is fresh moonlight bottled in green.
        You slip your fingers further from the
noise,
As if some things
Are only supposed to be loved from a distance.

What am I to do with this version of love?
When the present deafens you,
And yet I want to fall into it—

Rapture//

I have seen
how the waves
    s o f t e n
at the mere mention
      of your name.

On the cusp of a daydream,
I am the sand
that cannot help being dragged
      towards you—
The kind trapped inside an hourglass.

Betwixt the Pages//

If we were books sandwiched between
whimsical titles and back cover summaries,
we'd read each other in the far corner of the
third floor of a library that we've never been to
on a Wednesday afternoon
and by the end, our words would blend and
become the same – a simple retelling of the
other's name.

The Ballad of You and I//

And I cannot shape the words into the silhouette
of myself–
Only loose refrains remain.
But the thoughts do not leave me
Like a song stuck in the mind to which the lyrics
evade capture.
Our vocal cords have become too narrow
To fit the both of us.
Any noise simply evaporates into the echo
Of a conversation we never had.
Perhaps it is you—

Man in the Moon//

We looked up from our musings like
overzealous dreamers
Brought here to capture the sunset; but it never
shone.
A cage and key would be of little use
For the shivering moon. In it,
We saw only immeasurable figures,
That of a man, with vibrant eyes of glacial topaz.

Asymmetry//

morning
    traffic

only wonder
   lost to
buzzing engines

  against the azure
skylarks
     dip
and trill something
I cannot touch

I'm shaping
my world without
being able
   to fully build it

Paper Chains//

12

Last night
I tore out all the poems I wrote about you
And made them into paper chains.
Looping the past with those jagged edges
blurred the words
Until they were little more than petty decoration.
In the morning the pages were clear,
Shaken from the shackles with glue that could
not hold.

Medicine for Heartache//

Their love was a wild berry tea,
rich and gentle but
steeped too-long in a papery encasement.
And while the cup was filled,
steam clouded vision
　　　　heralded stormy waves
　　　　　　which rolled across the
　　　porcelain.
As they drank,
the soft liquid stained the room a muddy pink.
To finish the cup would be to taste the rotten
dregs sour.

Abstraction//

A vowel too redundant stays inside the seams of
substance
Thoughtful in its nearness
Begging to forget the very nature of itself.
And any sound you make, inhale, remains right
there out of context.
I wonder at the taste of forgotten nothings
      Loose ends
           Unfinished jottings
They call on me for late hours after midnight
Wishing they didn't know how to morph a maze
into silence.
J'espère que les mots vous reviendront.
But fever is a bad dream.

Wild//

I am no overgrown garden
daring
to breach my boundaries

my weeds run deep
          strong
as those that have been bruised will survive
against the elements.
Do not think to test these limits
with harsh hands or sharp blades.

This jungle in me cannot be tamed—

Woman//

Today feels like the colour
Like the dream that dared to drift but never
reach.
Today is a place where stone walls
Are nought but renditions
Of sugary daylight hours. Here
We can coat the minutes in daisy chains
And set the roads in reverse.
Permission cannot be gained to smash such glass
ceilings.
The world is a peach, and we are daring to bite
closer
to the bitter stone.

Billie Jean//

She caused a scene
that stirred up the very name of a sordid back
alley
into a perfect anagram of her own.
Laced with the smell of sweet perfume
and hiding nightmares in coat pockets,
her heels marched rhythms into the floorboards.
　　　　　Whisper now—
Silver slips through her fingers
as you part your lips.
The law was on her side, her schemes and plans
unbound.

Daydreaming in Auburn//

Watch the greens blush in crimson hues,
      drunk off summer's waned warmth.

Kisses on windburned cheeks
are stained with autumn's whispers, and yet
Still–
I betray the curtains and pull them back too soon
from the buttery sun.
Leaves
The colour of her eyes
Are wakened by the crispness of the October
morn,
The muddied pathways,
The candied fog.
The world reflected in a single raindrop,
carrying her smile.

Keep these moments between the pages
They are not pressed leaves,
They will not crumble.

Falling Through Puddles//

[I]
The lights of the cars are pixelated in the rain
I never meant to sit beside you –
you still make room.

[II]
You're holding an umbrella over my head
Because I always forget mine on rainy days and
you know it.
For a momentary glimpse in time
I allow myself to appreciate the
Way your freckles fall across your cheeks
Like brown sugar tossed with a careless hand.
My damp shivers soften with you.

[III]
It rains like that again today
And it is blue and cold and
All the weak adjectives you find in a
second-hand shop.
I think of how we ignored our sodden feet,
And of how the rain turned your eyes
opalescent.
You pick me up with an umbrella in hand.

While//

Strike the moon like a match head against the
sky
Until it erupts into morning
And we can once again
Pour quick seasons through our fingertips.

We're only borrowing this starlight for a breath
of time,
And you swallowed the hesitation long before I
could tie it
with the ribbon we found.
The hands don't pause for us, nor the sand still.

Each night tortures when you remember
The aching dullness of an afternoon's amber;
The fullness of blurred memories;
The empty space where we whispered our
existence
Without being noticed.
      I'm surprised to see how the years look
on our bodies.

Theory of Relative Disillusion//

I hold out my hand
to the empty night sky
and ask
for a star to fall from the velvet nothing.
Finally,
I might have the courage to wish—
maybe then
you'd see me bursting into my own colour.